3.99

GW00671279

BUNGAY CASTLE

Historical Notes
and
Account of the Excavations

by

HUGH BRAUN, F.R.I.B.A., F.S.A.

with a memoir by

Dr. HUGH CANE, M.B., B.CH.

Published for
BUNGAY CASTLE TRUST
by
Morrow & Co., Bungay, Suffolk

First published in the Proceedings of the
Suffolk Institute of Archaelogy & Natural History
1934 and 1935

First published in book form
for Bungay Castle Trust Ltd 1991
by Morrow & Co., Bungay, Suffolk 1991

ISBN 0 948903 11 2

Set and printed in Bungay by Bungay Printers, Bungay, Suffolk
and bound by Crowes of Norwich

Contents

Illustrations

Acknowledgement

The publisher would like to thank Mr. & Mrs. D. Bettiss, Dr. L. H. Cane, Mr. J. V. Cowan, Mr. S. Leahy and Mr. C. Reeve for help given in the production of this book.

It is to be sold for the benefit of Bungay Castle Trust whose prime object is the repair of Bungay Castle to ensure its preservation for future generations.

HUGH STANLEY BRAUN, F.R.I.B.A., F.S.A.
1902–1974
A Memoir by Dr. Hugh Cane, M.B., B.CH.

In 1934 when my father, Dr. Leonard Cane, as Town Reeve, engaged Mr. Hugh Braun to direct the excavation of Bungay Castle he was a little-known architect with an interest in archaeology. Nevertheless, he had been to Iraq only the previous year with the Chicago University Expedition to excavate the ruins of Nineveh. Later on he was to visit Malta to research into their ancient civilisation and architecture.

During his life he became well-known as an author of books on architecture, notably *Old London Buildings, Historical Architecture, Parish Churches, Cathedral Architecture, The Story of the English House, English Abbeys* and *Maltese Architecture*. His first and best known book *The English Castle* was published in 1936, the year following his work in Bungay. It had a foreword by Hilaire Belloc and went into three editions.

When he was working on Bigod's Castle in Bungay he was based in London and travelled here by train at weekends, staying with us in Trinity Street. He was then still a bachelor but later married a widow who had a young daughter: they had no children of their own. As far as I know he never charged a penny for his work at the castle though we found him some remuneration designing the Flixton Road Council Estate. He also designed for the Town Trust the Black Dog Lamp Standard in the Market Place which replaced the old Town Pump. The layout of the Castle Hills, recently acquired by the Trust, was also his work, including the design of the wrought-iron Bigod gates. As a result of his research into the early history of the Bigods and their buildings he invented the Town Reeve's civic flag to fly from the ruins. It depicts a red lion on a green and yellow background.

After the war Hugh Braun settled in Marlborough where he continued his architectural practice. I last met him in Bungay a year before his death at the age of 72. I know he was gratified that we had continued to care for the castle ruins and that the Suffolk County Council had purchased the derelict saleground opposite and restored it as part of the Inner Bailey. He took a great interest in Bungay and we were fortunate to have had his expert advice.

HUGH STANLEY BRAUN, F.R.I.B.A., F.S.A.

PART I

Some Notes on

BUNGAY CASTLE

By H<small>UGH</small> B<small>RAUN</small>, F.S.A., A.R.I.B.A.

T HE town of Bungay occupies what is perhaps one of the most remarkable sites in this country. The River Waveney, pursuing a more or less direct course easterly from Diss towards the sea, on approaching the site of Bungay meets a spur of high ground thrusting northwards from Suffolk and diverting the stream to the north. From this point the river describes an immense loop round what is called Outney Common and, turning again southwards, resumes its easterly route to Beccles and the sea. From the point where the divergence takes place to that where the orderly course is resumed is but a few hundred yards across and this isthmus, at the base of Suffolk's far flung peninsular of Outney, is the site of Bungay town. Its flanks slope abruptly to the river, and protected by these scarps and the marshes at their foot, Bungay stands on a site which might almost be described as a natural fortress, accessible only at either end towards Outney and the Suffolk mainland.

The addition of two lines of defence across these unprotected ends of the isthmus would make the site an exceedingly formidable stronghold and it is therefore not in the least surprising to find that this has in fact been made by some early occupants of the settlement. Remains of the northern line may be seen in the deep ditch of which portions remain in the goods yard of the railway station, and the line of the southern rampart may also be seen on the northern side of Quaves Lane. This thoroughfare runs at the edge of the town ditch and it may be noticed that the two Olland Streets converge at the site of the south gate of the town.

One may speculate as to the probable period at which these defences were constructed. They are not apparently the work of prehistoric peoples and the site is hardly one which would appeal to the Roman especially as his road passed a mile or so to the eastward. The ditches probably existed in Saxon days, as the manor was known at the time of the Domesday survey by the name of Bungay Burgh, which latter word denotes a fortified town. It may have been the Saxons who first constructed the earthwork fortifications of Bungay as a defence against the Danish raiders or even the Danes themselves as a base for the protection of themselves and their Waveney-borne long-ships during the enforced idleness of an East Anglian winter.

It seems certain that at the time of the Norman conquest Bungay was a very important town. In Domesday Book, its entries occupy far more than their fair share of the Suffolk portion. After the Conquest was completed, Bungay was still in Saxon hands, being part of the estates of Stigand, the Saxon archbishop of Canterbury, whose wise surrender to the new regime had prevented the forfeiture of his property with that of most of the other Saxon landowners. Stigand was able to continue thus favoured for four years after the Conquest, but by 1070 William seems to have found that his assistance could be dispensed with and an excuse was found to depose him and deprive him of his estates, including the town of Bungay. The lands thus acquired were put out to farm by William and Bungay fell to the lot of William de Noyers, one of the less well-provided for of the King's Norman followers.

If we consider the position of this man, an usurper taking possession of a large and important town, doubtless proud of its survival as a Saxon borough in the midst of a conquered country, we shall see at once that his position was an unenviable one. If he was going to live in the place, he would need a more defensible residence than the usual timber hall of the period. It was probably William de Noyers, therefore, who followed the usual Norman custom of raising a mound-castle in the centre of the town, deeply ditched about and with its summit strongly palisaded to form an effective protection for his timber house against such efforts as might be attempted by his Saxon tenants to burn his home over his head while he and his household slept. The summit of the mound would have been approached by a timber bridge, sloping upwards over the western side of the ditch. The foot of this bridge itself would need to be protected from possible burning by an enemy and was thus defended by a small ditched and mounded barbican

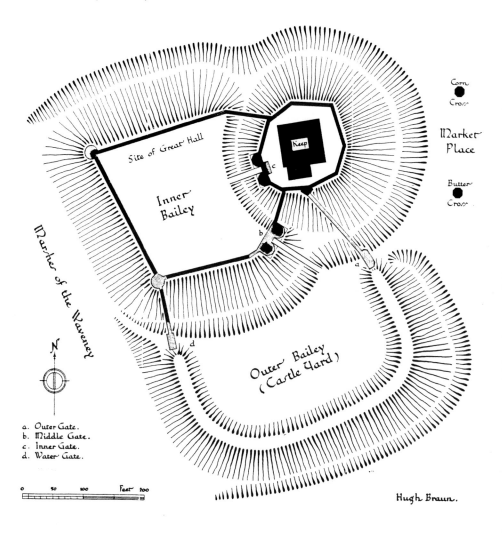

Bungay Castle.
Restored Plan.

Suffolk.

Corn
Cross

Market
Place

Butter
Cross

Site of Great Hall

Keep

Inner
Bailey

Marshes of the Waveney

N

Outer Bailey
(Castle Yard)

a. Outer Gate.
b. Middle Gate.
c. Inner Gate.
d. Water Gate.

0   50   100   Feet 200

Hugh Braun.

Fig. I — Restored Plan

between the castle itself and the western scarps above the river. This barbican is now the Bungay Stock Mart and was until recently a bowling green.

It is not known how long William de Noyers held Bungay for the king but he was in possession at the time of the Domesday survey of 1086 and may have continued to hold it until the death of William Rufus in 1100. Soon after the accession of Henry I, however, we find that Bungay has changed hands, having been in 1103 bestowed on Roger Bigod,[1] one of the few great Norman magnates who had assisted the new king in seizing the throne when the arrow of Walter Tirel had removed its previous occupant. Together with Bungay, Roger received the nearby manor of Framlingham[2] and it seems highly probably that it was he who, possibly dissatisfied with the little mound-castle of William de Noyers at Bungay, raised the huge earthwork which is now crowned by the lofty walls of Framlingham Castle. Nothing is known of Roger Bigod's sojourn as castellan of Bungay, if indeed he ever resided there, and he would seem to have lived only a few years after his receiving the grants, for he died, it is believed, in 1107.[3] If this be so, he would have been succeeded by his young son, William, who, however, is known to have perished, together with the heir to the throne and many another gallant young Norman lord, in the great disaster of November, 1120,[4] when the fair white ship went down off the cliffs of Barfleur.

It was this disaster, which gave to Bungay its most famous lord and castellan, Hugh Bigod, Bigod the Restless, the Bold Bigod. While his benefactor lived he seems to have been content to remain tranquil and establish his position as virtual lord of East Anglia, but as soon as Henry was dead he showed his hand by ungratefully deserting Henry's daughter, the Empress, and giving his strong support to the usurper Stephen.[5] It is clear that, throughout his career, Hugh was one who believed in supporting his own, that is the winning cause, for, in 1136, on a rumour that Stephen was dead, Hugh seized the royal castle of Norwich and garrisoned it for himself, the king having to march an army to the place before Bigod would give it up.[6]

Four years later he again rebelled, this time making Bungay his headquarters, but "In 1140, at Pentecost, the king with his army came upon Hugo Bigod of Suffolk and took the castle of Bunie."[7] Two months later, however, Bigod broke out again and Stephen

BUNGAY CASTLE SUFFOLK
Plan of Motte as excavated: May 1935.

Hugh Braun, F.S.A.
mens. et delt:

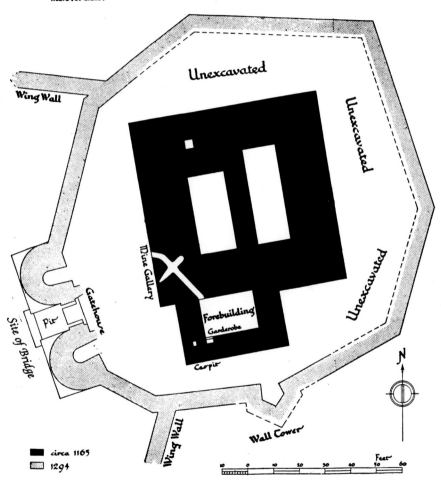

Unexcavated

Unexcavated

Unexcavated

Unexcavated

Wing Wall

Mine Gallery

Gatehouse

Pit

Site of Bridge

Forebuilding

Garderobe

Cesspit

Wing Wall

Wall Tower

N

circa 1165
1294

Feet
10 0 10 20 30 40 50 60

FIG. II — PLAN OF MOTTE AS EXCAVATED, MAY 1935.

again was forced to march against him, but this time tried the expedient of giving him an earldom to keep him quiet.[8] This seems to have been just what Bigod needed, and thus in 1141 we find the new Earl of the East Angles fighting in the foremost line of battle for his sovereign lord the king at Lincoln field.[9] Unfortunately for Stephen, however, the battle turned against him, and he, with most of his captains, left the field a prisoner. Hugh Bigod had retired earlier on observing how matters were proceeding, and thus escaped capture. Next year he is on the side of the Empress Matilda,[10] and nine years later, in 1150, he is still found to be on the popular side.[11] In the summer of 1153, Stephen besieged him in Ipswich and succeeded in turning him out, but Matilda's young son, the future Henry II, was already showing that prowess which was to distinguish him throughout his reign, and the unhappy king, worn out with the twenty years of dreadful strife which had accompanied his tenure of the throne of England, was nearly at the end of his resources and before a year had passed his reign was over and the son of his rival, hailed by most of the country, firmly seated in his stead.

The new king, although but twenty-one years of age, was already a seasoned warrior when he came to the throne. He showed his strength immediately by putting down with a firm hand the unruly barons who for twenty years had kept the country plunged in the miseries of anarchy. Among these was Hugh Bigod, who was deprived of his castles,[13] although he was allowed to retain his harmless title as Earl of Norfolk.[14] By 1163, however, Henry seems to have considered Bigod sufficiently chastened for it to be safe to give him back his castles, which he therefore did.[15] Bigod replied by fortifying that of Bungay so strongly that he felt safe within its walls to defy Henry for all time to turn him out again. It seems highly probable that it was at this period that the great square keep was constructed, as this possesses definite affinity with that of the castle at Scarborough, which Henry began to build in 1157 and finished about 1174.[16] Moreover, in 1165, which may perhaps be about the time when Bungay keep was commenced, we find Henry founding what would seem, from the Pipe Rolls relating to it, to be one of his favourite castles, that of Orford, obviously intended to keep Bigod and his Flemish mercenary adherents in check as far as possible.

Orford keep took seven years to build, having been finished about 1172,[17] and it is doubtful whether the immense structure at Bungay could have been completed much earlier. At any rate, when

FIG. III — THE GATEHOUSE BEFORE EXCAVATION.

FIG. IV — LOOKING TOWARDS THE KEEP THROUGH THE EXCAVATED GATEHOUSE.

rebellion broke out all over Normandy and England during the Easter of 1173, Bigod seems to have had no hesitation in joining in with the revolting barons against the king.[18] One of the leaders of the rebellion was the Earl of Leicester, who had gone over to Normandy to assist the rebels there but finding that Henry had already got them well in hand returned to England with an army of Flemish mercenaries in the October of 1173 and laid siege to the King's castle of Walton,[19] which — long since vanished "down cliff" — then stood in the north-east angle of the old Roman fort. The well manned and provisioned stronghold[20] held out and four days of siege convinced Leicester that he could not afford to waste time over its reduction, so he marched to Framlingham to join forces with Hugh Bigod. The two then marched on the royal castle of Haughley, which fell after four days' siege during the first week in November. The two contented earls then returned to Framlingham, possibly intending to celebrate Christmas within its walls, but Leicester, finding that his army of Flemings was too great a strain on the resources of his hosts, decided to leave and make for his own city. To his dismay he found that two of the royal barons, whom he had thought were in the North, had marched southwards and were lying in wait for him at Bury St. Edmunds with a force of 300 mercenaries. The Earl tried to give them the slip but was caught as he was fording the river Lark at Fornham St. Genevieve. One charge of the royal army settled the affair. The Earl's little force was annihilated and he with his wife and most of his captains captured and sent to prison in Normandy.[21]

This battle took place about the 16th November, 1173, but, despite the blow it must have been to Bigod and the corresponding spur to the royalists, nothing seems to have been done to bring him to terms except a rather futile truce made with him by the King, the only terms of which were that Bigod was to dismiss some of his Flemish mercenaries. One cannot but admire the diplomacy of the tough old Earl when we read that the King agreed to conduct them to Dover and have them thence shipped home *at his own expense!*[22]

The truce was to last until May 19th, but unfortunately for the cause of Peace, an army of Flemings, 418 strong, landed in the Orwell and placed themselves under the command of Bigod, who at once besieged Dunwich. Unsuccessful for once, they turned to Norwich, which was betrayed to them by internal treachery on the 18th June.[23] The King was at this time in Normandy, but on the 8th

FIG. V — THE WEST WALL OF THE KEEP AND ITS INTERIOR.

July he crossed to England, arriving at Canterbury on the 12th to do penance at the shrine of Becket. Two days later he was in London and on the 18th he had started with an army for East Anglia. Huntingdon surrendered on the 21st and the 24th saw him encamped at Syleham near Diss[24] where he began with a great army of carpenters, five hundred strong,[25] to prepare siege engines for the reduction of Bungay castle. Up to this time, the principle form of siege weapon had been the small *mangon* worked by tension or torsion and having a low trajectory and a short range of fire, but Henry during his sojourn abroad may have learnt of the giant catapult or *trébuchet* which worked by counterpoise and hurled immense projectiles in a high arc over the highest walls. The first recorded use of these formidable weapons in this country is at the siege of Dover in 1216, but they were certainly employed on the Continent before this time and it may have been that Henry's five hundred carpenters were engaged in making them, for the first time in this country, at Syleham in the summer of 1174.

Whatever it was they were doing, however, there can be no doubt that it at last put fear into the heart of Hugh Bigod, for, before twenty-four hours had elapsed he had left Bungay and come to terms with Henry at Syleham. The interview was brief; the terms were unconditional for the Earl. Neither he nor the King left their saddles during the interview and in a few minutes Bigod was an outlawed traitor.[26] The Flemings were disbanded and sent home, this time probably "carriage forward." Bigod's castles were ordered to be destroyed and he himself disgraced.[27]

The great castle of Framlingham was almost entirely destroyed. Its palisades were thrown down and about a quarter of the eastern side of the great mound thrown back into the ditch whence it had been raised. The royal engineer, Alnodus of Ipswich, who had just completed Orford Castle, was called into effect the demolition,[28] and it may be assumed that it was he also who commenced the destruction of Bungay Castle by driving the mine gallery across the foundations of the south-west angle of its keep. It appears, however, that Bigod ransomed the great tower by paying one thousand marks,[29] which probably represents more than fifteen thousand pounds sterling, and it may be for this reason that we have had the good fortune to find that the mine system was left unfinished and thus can appreciate the intention of its designer.

The surrender of Hugh Bigod seems to have broken the back of

Fig. VI — The South-west Corner of the Keep and the Forebuilding.

the rebellion for good, within a week the remainder of the disloyal barons had surrendered and peace restored once more. Two years or so later, Bigod the Restless, battle-weary, found peace at last; fighting to the end in distant Syria.[30]

Hugh Bigod's son, Roger, did not come into his heritage during the lifetime of the king who had suffered so much from his father's turbulence,* but the next king, Richard I, was not long in restoring him to his estates, returning them, for a consideration of yet another thousand marks, as soon as he came to the throne in 1189.[31] Roger does not seem to have done anything to Bungay Castle, probably because he concentrated all his efforts in building, on the larger and completely cleared site, the huge castle of Framlingham, which he erected in the very latest fashion, keep-less but with lofty, many-towered curtain walls for defence against the great catapults which were coming into fashion.

Framlingham Castle continued to be the chief seat of the Bigods and their successors from this time onwards and Bungay's history fades into the background before the splendour of its neighbour. Roger married Isobel Plantagenet and their son Hugh succeeded his father in 1215, at a time when King John was honouring Framlingham Castle with his presence. Hugh married Maud, daughter of William Marshal, the great Earl of Pembroke, and, dying in 1225, was succeeded by their son Roger, who married Isobel, sister of the King of Scots, but died without issue in 1269.

The line then changed, and Roger's nephew, his namesake, became the fifth Earl of Norfolk. This Roger was the son of his uncle Roger's brother Hugh, by his second marriage with Joan Stuteville.[32] This change to a collateral succession seems to have brought out all the characteristics of the Bigod blood, Roger from the beginning trying to live up to the reputation of his ancestor the Bold Bigod. The stories told of his defiance against the royal authority are too well known to be related here. The interest attaching to him in connection with Bungay Castle is that he seems at last to have taken it in hand, obtaining in 1294 a licence to crenellate his "house" of

---

*It seems quite possible that, after the disgrace of Hugh Bigod, Bungay may have been given by Henry to Roger, brother of his great Justiciar, Ranulf de Glanville, for about the year 1188 (not 1160, as incorrectly stated by Dudgale) Roger of Glanville, who had meanwhile married Gundrada, Bigod's widow, founded at Bungay the Priory of St. Mary, some remains of which, including the nave of the Priory Church, now the Parish Church of St. Mary, are still to be seen. See *Geoffrey de Mandeville*, Round, p. 318.

FIG. VII — THE SITE OF THE FORE-BUILDING BEFORE EXCAVATION.

FIG. VIII — THE EXCAVATED FORE-BUILDING SHOWING THE MINE GALLERY.

"Bungeye."[33] It would seem that its use as a castle had lapsed after the surrender of 1174. It is doubtless as a result of obtaining his licence that the existing lofty curtain walls were built, not only round the original mound but also to the little barbican bailey, outside the two-towered gatehouse, which is of this period also. There was another gatehouse of approximately the same design through which the barbican bailey was approached from the huge outer bailey or Castle Yard, surrounded by the mighty ramparts of the Castle Hills, which were probably thrown up by Hugh Bigod the Restless at the same time as he built the keep. The style of the work of 1294 is similar to that which was being done by the king himself in various parts of the country at this time, notably on the Welsh marches as at Conway and Harlech.

Roger thus completed a fine new castle, retaining, however, the original keep of Hugh Bigod, which he appears to have re-faced — it had probably been used as a quarry for over a century — and also to have made the four windows on the ground floor, two and a half of which may still be seen. Scarcely was his work finished, however, when his stormy life came to an end in 1297, he having made restitution to his often outraged sovereign by leaving all his estates to the Crown. He had been married twice, once to Olivia Basset and a second time to Alicia or Aleyde of Hainault,[34] but neither had given him children. His heir would have been his brother John, who had, however, persisted in dunning him for money borrowed by the elder brother, who had therefore achieved his revenge by disinheriting the importunate offender.[35] The unfortunate John died in 1300, when his uncle John, younger brother of Roger the fourth Earl, attempted to recover the lost estates, but, being unsuccessful, was forced to fly the country and find refuge in Hainault.[36]

In 1312, Edward II gave Bungay to his brother, Thomas Plantagenet, surnamed de Brotherton, Earl Marshal of England, to whom Edward I, his father, had already given Framlingham. On Thomas's death the castle passed to a daughter and thenceforth passed through many different hands, finally becoming the property of the Howards in 1483.[37]

Thomas de Brotherton's daughter Alice had carried Bungay to her husband Edward of Montacute and their daughter Joan, born in 1348, brought the castle her birthplace to her husband William de Ufford, Earl of Suffolk in 1362, but he, possibly preferring to live in his great castle of Haughley nearby, allowed Bungay Castle to

Fig. IX — The Garderobe in the South-west Corner of the
Fore-building, showing the Original Wooden Seat in Position.

become ruinous. At his death in 1382 it is returned as both old and ruinous.

There is some indication that the castle was occupied and perhaps even repaired during the fifteenth century, possibly during the troublous period of the Wars of the Roses, but its day ended, to all intents, with the death of Edward de Montacute in 1362.

The Howards, lords of Arundel and Framlingham, could never have had much use for the deserted ruins of Bungay Castle, and it is perhaps not surprising to find that in 1766 it was sold to an inhabitant of Bungay, a Mr. Mickleborough, who intended to take it down and sell the stones as road metal. He set men to work on it with picks, and to this day can be seen the depredations they wrought, undermining the walls of the keep until they had brought down the south-west angle which had been preserved from the previous assaults of Alnodus of Ipswich at such heavy cost to the pocket of Hugh Bigod its builder. Fortunately for posterity, the masonry was so strong that Mr. Mickleborough's workmen broke all their picks before they had completely removed the castle, and the destructive gentleman found it would not pay him to continue. He therefore sold what remained to the wife of a resident of Bungay, a Mrs. Bonhote, who converted the gatehouse into a residence by building a cottage between its two towers, in which she lived and wrote books, notably the two-volume novel "Bungay Castle."

About 1800 she sold it back to the Dukes of Norfolk, who seemed at last to be realising that their heritage was slipping away from them. Unfortunately a lapse occurred when in 1884 the trustees of the Norfolk estates sold it again to the Bungay Lodge of Oddfellows, who built a large brick hall against the eastern side of the mound. In 1898, however, it was again rescued by the Duke of Norfolk, whose son has retained it to the present day.

During the centuries which had elapsed since the castle had been in use as a residence its condition had been steadily becoming worse. It had of course been used as a quarry for building material throughout, and much of it, the outer and middle gatehouses, for example, had vanished completely. Cottages and hovels had been erected against the walls and rubbish of all descriptions dumped in and about the ruins. Recently the keep and its surroundings had been used as a beer-garden, and the castle was usually described in guide-books as being "in the yard of the King's Head Inn."

In 1933, when the Feoffees of Bungay began to take notice of the forlorn condition of their castle, all that could be seen of it was two ivy-covered towers and a few snags of walling rising from a jungle of coarse vegetation and chicken wire and garrisoned by an army of scratching fowls. Under the leadership of their energetic Town Reeve, Dr. Leonard B. Cane, the Feoffees approached the Duke of Norfolk to endeavour to obtain a lease of the Castle to the town and after much negotiation they were successful. As a preliminary the poultry were ejected and the ruins cleared of ivy. An appeal for subscriptions was issued and met with a surprising result, money coming in from all over the world to assist in the preservation of the famous castle of the Bold Bigod, until within a few months half the sum of £500 appealed for had been subscribed.

Archaeological supervision was procured and on November 19th, 1934, the Town Reeve of Bungay cut the first sod of the excavation work which was to provide employment for otherwise unemployed ex-Service men for several months at least.

A start was made by clearing the space between the keep ruins and the gatehouse of the five feet or so of accumulated debris, and the plan of the great keep itself and its hitherto undiscovered forebuilding was soon recovered. The surprising discovery was made that the whole of the mound had been raised, at some period subsequent to the erection of the keep, with some twelve feet of fine gravel which was thus burying the lower portion of all the Norman walls. It was at once appreciated that if this accretion could be cleared away, the result would be a great improvement in the appearance of the castle, as the buried walls were uninjured and if exposed would show the castle rising some twenty feet higher than before excavation commenced. On the other hand, it was realised that the discovery would add enormously to the cost of the work if full advantage were taken of it.

For the present, therefore, it was decided to sink an exploratory shaft down the south-west angle of the keep to sound the thickness of the gravel and expose the stepped base of the great tower. This done, the gatehouse was freed from the remains of Mrs. Bonhote's cottage and the drawbridge pit exposed to view. The west wall of the keep was then cleared, as well as the two chambers within it, which were excavated down to the top of the gravel layer with which they, too, were filled. The whole of the interior of the tower was filled with fallen masses of wall and several other enormous portions of the fallen west wall of the keep were found to be lying on the gravel between it and the gatehouse, effectively preventing further excavation until they could be removed with explosives. The newly discovered forebuilding, however, being free from such hindrances, was excavated down to its original floor. At the time of going to Press, the available money having been used up, the excavations are being tidied up preparatory to being turfed and in that condition they will be left until the accumulation of further funds permits further exploration.

The soil taken from the excavations has been used to fill in the huge quarries made in the ramparts of the outer bailey by the local authority some years ago when material was needed for the repair of roads. These "Castle Hills" are like the Castle itself, also scheduled as an ancient monument so we are perhaps exceptionally fortunate in being able to repair one part of the Castle with the material taken from another.

Visitors to the Castle to-day should approach it through the narrow passage from St. Mary's Street at a point almost opposite the west door of St. Mary's Church. This passage represents the site of the bridge over the ditch of the outer bailey and at its further end from the street is the site of the outer gatehouse. This spot just within the outer gate is known as Castle Orchard. The visitor is now within the outer bailey or Castle Yard, the remains of the huge ramparts of which may be discerned in front and to the left of a person standing in Castle Orchard with his back to the passage just described.

Should he turn to the right round the cottages of Castle Orchard and enter Castle Lane, the visitor will be traversing the site of the bridge over the ditch of the inner or barbican bailey and half way along the lane, will pass, by a cottage, the site of the middle gatehouse, the foundations of which have been discovered beneath the lane and its adjoining gardens. If he will turn, immediately opposite the twin towers, and cross the intervening space, he will then be traversing the site of the permanent bridge across the now filled-in ditch which surrounded the mound of the original castle. His way will then be barred by the drawbridge pit between the gatehouse towers.[38] The last pier of the permanent bridge may be seen just in front of the towers and at the sides of the pit he may see the holes which carried the pivot of the balanced bridge, at the inner end of the pit being the slots for the counterpoise arms.

Within the site of the lofty curtain-wall of 1294, portions of which may be seen around,* stand the ruins of the great keep of circa 1165.

This great tower, seventy feet square externally, is about the same size as the keep of Rochester in Kent, and thus comes about sixteenth in size amongst the seventy-five known rectangular keeps in this country. While thus not quite the largest keep in the country, it is second to none as regards the thickness of its wall, which are eighteen feet through, while one half of the north wall is twenty-three feet thick, probably the thickest wall in this country. The thirty-four feet span of the keep internally is too great for a timber floor-beam, so the interior is divided by a cross-wall, eight feet thick, running north and south, a door cut through it connecting the two halves of the keep. The usual place for the staircase in early keeps is at one of the angles, but Bungay keep has a staircase in the centre of the north wall, a feature which it shares with only one other great tower, that of Scarborough, built between 1157 and 1174. This perhaps assists one in arriving at an estimate of the date of Bungay keep. On a mezzanine floor in the north-west angle is a garderobe having a shaft which descends to forty feet below the present surface of the ground. The ground floor had four narrow, deeply splayed windows, which at present show thirteenth century heads, as does the little light in the north-west side of the stair. The head of the north-west window of the keep was found among the fragments littering the interior. The stair does not now descend to the ground floor, having been turned into a fireplace at some later date, as have the staircases at Norwich keep. There is no sign of a stair from the ground floor to the basement, nor does any sign remain as to how the ground floor joists were supported. The fall of one of the huge pieces of walling had badly damaged the south-west angle of the keep externally, and this has now been built up again by the present excavators.

Attached to the south wall of the keep is a large forebuilding or entrance tower, thirty-eight feet long and twenty-two broad with walls eight feet thick, the largest in this country save that of Portchester in Hampshire. Its walls are honeycombed with curious holes, the purpose of which has not yet been ascertained. In the south-west angle is a garderobe, the slots for the wooden seat being visible in the walling beside the opening. The oak seat itself was

---

*To the south of the keep may be seen the lower part of a curious wall-tower of unusual plan, this being a half-hexagon, open at the gorge. This tower would appear to stand at the junction of the rampart of the outer bailey with that of the inner curtain.

found on the floor nearby. Beneath the garderobe is a vaulted cess-
pit, seven feet by five, the excavation of which had to be stopped
when the depth of forty feet below the ground had been reached.
Alongside the garderobe a shaft from a similar one on a now
vanished upper floor may be seen.

In the north-west angle of the forebuilding may be seen what is
believed to be the unfinished mine of 1174. This is a gallery, twenty-
six feet long, cutting across the angle of the keep and having two
incomplete lateral galleries leaving it near its centre.

The keep has been destroyed above its entrance floor, so that no
hope can be entertained of ever discovering the entrance, but it is to
be hoped that some future date may see the area outside the east
face of the forebuilding cleared and the external stair which may
possibly exist there fully exposed.

If the visitor will stand between the twin towers of the gateway
and look outwards towards the river he will be looking over the site
of the inner bailey, the walls of which still survive for the most part,
although sections have fallen outwards into the ditches at their foot.
In this enclosure were once the domestic buildings of the castle, its
great hall, kitchens, bowers and chapel. One day it is hoped to
examine this bailey for the foundations of buildings which are
known to exist under the turf, showing through occasionally during dry summers.

For the present, however, we must be content with the tidying up
which has been effected and which has enabled visitors more easily
to appreciate the ancient grandeur of the great tower of Bungay, the
raison d'etre perhaps for the boast of the Bold Bigod —

> "Were I in my Castle of Bungaye
> Above the Water of Waveney,
> I would ne care for the King of Cockneye,
> And all his meiny*!"

*Pronounced "mainy" and meaning "retinue".

NOTES

1. *The Castles of England*. Mackenzie, Vol. I, p. 272.
2. *Ibid*. p. 278.
3. *Ibid*.
4. *Ibid*.
5. *Gesta 7–9, de Diceto*, etc.
6. *Ann. Waverley*.
7. *Ibid*.
8. *Ibid*.
9. William of Malmesbury.
10. *Geoffrey de Mandeville*, Round. p. 165–172.
11. *Foundations of England*, Ramsay. Vol. II, p. 441.
12. *Ibid*. p. 450.
13. Mackenzie, *sup*. p. 272.
14. *The Angevin Empire*. Ramsay, p. 5.
15. Mackenzie. *sup*.
16. Pipe Rolls.
17. *Ibid*.
18. *de Diceto*, etc.
19. *Ibid*.
20. Pipe Roll.
21. *de Diceto*.
22. *Ibid*.
23. *Ibid*.
24. *Benedictus*.
25. Pipe Roll.
26. *Benedictus*.
27. *de Diceto*.
28. *Pipe Rolls*.
29. *Mackenzie*. sup. p. 273.
30. *Ibid*.
31. *Ibid*.
32. For this and much other information concerning the Bigod Earls of Norfolk, I am indebted to a letter from M. Paul Bigot of Turenne, descendant of the disinherited John. *inf*.
33. Patent Roll.
34. M. Paul Bigot. *sup*.
35. Mackenzie. *sup*. p. 273.
36. M. Paul Bigot. *sup*.
37. For a comprehensive table showing the descent of the Bigod castles see *Castles of England*, Evans, p. 335.
38. At the time of going to Press, the drawbridge pit has only been cleared to the depth of a foot or so, as until a bridge can be procured, further excavation would bar access between the towers. It is hoped, however, when work on it is continued, that traces may be discovered of an earlier gatehouse contemporary with the great keep, the central position of which would render desirable the provision of a stone gatehouse to protect the entrance.

PART II

Report on the Excavations on

BUNGAY CASTLE

By Hugh Braun, f.s.a., f.r.i.b.a.

FOLLOWING my notes on the history of Bungay Castle, which appeared in the last part of the Proceedings of the Suffolk Institute of Archæology, I now have the honour to present a report on the results of the examination of the site carried out during the period November, 1934, to July, 1935, at which time the funds collected had been exhausted. About £460 had been collected for the purpose, mostly from private individuals, although the local societies had subscribed liberally, and a valuable grant of twenty guineas had been made by the Society of Antiquaries of London. Two-thirds of the funds had been spent on local labour, over £200 having been paid in wages to unemployed ex-Service men. Besides the tidying and excavation work which had been carried out, certain sums had been spent on repairs to the masonry, hedges to replace destroyed walls, protective fences, and a permanent timber bridge to replace the old "turning bridge" which had formerly spanned the bridge-pit between the twin towers of the Inner Gatehouse. The publicity given to the work at the Castle had attracted some hundreds of visitors during the summer of 1935 and the collecting boxes placed in the ruins had benefited correspondingly. Now that the Castle has been tidied up and made accessible, it is to be hoped that it will henceforth take its proper place as an important Ancient Monument, and will continue to be inspected by visitors to Bungay, who will, by their contributions, enable the ancient ruin to be maintained for the perpetual enjoyment of those who take interest in the old buildings of this country.

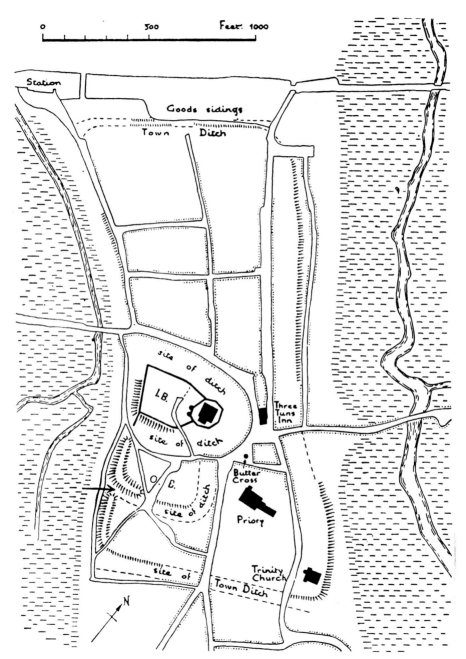

Fig. X — The Town of Bungay, showing the remains of its Mediaeval
Buildings and the traces of their Earthwork Defences.

THE EARTHWORKS

The site of the town of Bungay is a neck of high land, flanked to east and west by steep scarps rising above the swampy valley of the Waveney. At some period, possibly during the tenth century, the isthmus was fortified by cutting two entrenchments across from flank to flank, isolating the narrowest part of the site and forming a defensible site about three furlongs in length. At its narrowest point the site is about one furlong across from scarp to scarp. The flanks themselves appear to have been protected by earthen ramparts, in addition to the transverse entrenchments. Of the town's defences there still remain some portions of the northern entrenchment, somewhat complicated to-day by the cutting made by the railway company for their goods yard. The western half of the southern ditch is well seen from the lane known as Quaves Lane, which skirts its outer edge. At the back of the gardens on the north side of the lane may be seen the ramparts themselves. A fine stretch of rampart joins the south-west angle of the town to the earthworks of the Castle, the Outer Bailey of which was probably taken from the town. The western ramparts of the Castle are possibly part of the original town defences. The Town Plan (Fig. X) shows two streets, Upper and Lower Olland Streets, which meet at the edge of the ditch by the south gate of the town. From this point the main street of the ancient town appears to have run along the crest of the ridge, the market place being approximately half way between the south gate and one which may have led through the northern ramparts to the large river-protected common of Outney beyond.

The mound of the Norman castle was erected (possibly by William de Noyers in 1070) in the very centre of the town, the centre of the mound being almost exactly midway between the flanks of the isthmus.* The setting-out circle from which the mound was

*It may be of interest to note that the castle of Durham, founded by William the Conqueror in 1072, supplies a very close analogy with that of Bungay. At Durham, the old city is situated on a peninsular formed by a loop of the River Wear. At its narrowest part, the site is about a furlong across, as at Bungay. The castle mound, of almost exactly the same size as that at Bungay, is placed in the centre of this isthmus, the small barbican bailey being between the mound and the western scarps, as at Bungay.

At Norwich, where the city was situated in a rather wider loop of the River Wensum, the castle mound was again placed in the centre of the base of the loop. Here the river banks were too far off to be used as part of the defences of the bailey, so a small lunate enclosure was constructed to the south of the great mound, much larger than those of Bungay or Durham.

raised was struck at about a hundred foot radius, the whole mound with its ditch was about four hundred feet across at its widest part, and the area at the summit was originally about one hundred and fifty feet across, and raised about twenty feet above the level of the town below.

Between the mound and the western scarps a small bailey was set out about three hundred feet wide (about the distance from the centre of the mound to the edge of the cliff — perhaps this represents a hundred paces). It is at present not surrounded by ramparts, the whole area having been covered by the soil from the ditches. Possibly this was always so, or possibly the ramparts were removed when the stone walls were built. At present this bailey is about 250 feet across and 175 feet from the cliff to the original edge of the mound ditch. Its level is the same as that of the top of the mound.

At some period subsequent to its original foundation, the accommodation of the Castle was increased by the addition of an Outer Bailey. The subject of early Norman castles having been hitherto sadly neglected by archæologists, there is at present insufficient evidence to enable the probable period at which such additions may have been made to be stated with any degree of certainty. Possibly the addition was made when the garrison was augmented by Flemish mercenaries during the Anarchy of 1135–54. It would seem almost certain that the additional bailey must have been constructed not later than the time when the keep was built (circa 1164, v. inf.) as the consequent filling up of the summit of the original mound with this enormous tower must have forced the living accommodation of the castle into the Inner Bailey. The Outer Bailey would then have been needed for animals hitherto kept in the original bailey. The Outer Bailey at Bungay, called (probably from early times) Castle Yard, was set out along the southern side of the original castle, approximately two hundred feet away from the edges of the ditches. The earthwork appears to have been on an exceptionally large scale and must have encroached considerably on the area originally set out, leaving eventually a space some 150 feet across and twice as long.

The outer entrance to the Castle was where the eastern ramparts of the Outer Bailey reached the mound ditch (the passage beside the chemist's shop seems to represent this) and the way would then skirt the mound ditch into the Inner Bailey and thence to the timber bridge over the ditch into the area on the mound-top, arriving there, presumably at the point now marked by the twin-towered gate-house.

Of all this earthwork, practically only the river front of the Castle remains. The whole of the mound ditch has been filled in and much of it built upon. The same applies to the north ditch of the Inner Bailey, although its southern ditch may still be detected in the gardens which now cover it. The magnificent earthwork of the south-western angle of the Outer Bailey still remains to give some idea of the ancient strength of its defences (the soil removed from round the keep during the recent excavations was dumped into spoliatory quarries which had been made in these ramparts) and the whole of the run of the southern ramparts of this bailey can be detected among the gardens between the Council Yard and St. Mary's Street, the old High Street. The houses on the western side of this road have, however, completely obliterated the eastern ramparts of the Outer Bailey, the run of which can therefore only be conjectured.

EARLY BUILDINGS WITHIN THE CASTLE

The original accommodation of the castle would have consisted of a timber hall, probably rather like a mediæval barn, standing in the middle of the mound-top and surrounded by a stockade. The palisaded area of the original bailey would have contained stables and other outbuildings, also of timber.

The recent examination of the castle has shown, however, that the great keep was not the first stone structure on the mound. It was customary during the twelfth century to replace the early timber halls with either a stone hall or else a fortified structure or "hall-keep," such as at the Tower of London or Castle Rising. That there was no hall-keep at Bungay is shown by the fact of the existence of the present "tower-keep," a later type of structure which was a citadel rather than a residence. Built up into its walls, however, are a number of pieces of Caen stone which have obviously formed part of an earlier building, presumably an early stone hall. Inside the south wall of the forebuilding is built-in part of a slender column about eight inches in diameter and on the outer face of the west wall of the keep itself, near its north-west angle, is part of a moulded string-course (Fig. XIa) which suggests that the destroyed building belonged to the first half of the twelfth century. No more can be at present ascertained concerning this earlier hall, but if it is ever possible to clear out the interior of the keep to its foundations those of the earlier structure may then be found.

DESCRIPTION OF THE KEEP

The great tower stands on an "anti-mine" base about seventy feet square, the walls being at this level eighteen feet thick (Fig. XV). At about the present ground level, the exterior of the tower sloped back as a battering plinth (portions found, v. inf., see also Fig. XIII) about nine feet high until the faces of the walls were about five feet behind those of the base. This plinth has now entirely disappeared and its place is taken to-day by the undercutting effected in 1766 by a destructive gentleman who wished to overthrow the walls of the keep preparatory to breaking them up for road metal.

Above the site of the plinth may be seen, in the rough rubble masonry, a series of cracks representing the sites of the original pilasters which at one time ornamented the walls of the keep. These pilasters were each about thirteen feet wide and there would seem to have been one in the centre of each face as well as the usual pair at each angle. A careful examination of such portions of the original facings of the tower as remain to-day will demonstrate that the pilasters projected about two feet in front of the wall face.

There were found in the ruins a large number of quoins of Barnack stone which had formed part of an angle ornamented with a vertical shaft about eight inches in diameter. It may be that these quoins came from the angle of the keep, as the shafted angle is quite a common feature of tower keeps.

Internally the keep is about thirty-four feet square and this span, too great for a single floor beam, necessitated its division into two by a cross wall eight feet thick, leaving the two halves of the interior thirteen feet wide. The wall at the northern end of the west chamber has been thickened to twenty-three feet in order to provide room for the staircase, and the chamber has thus been shortened by five feet.

The strong foundation storey of the keep was apparently buried several feet deep in fine gravel taken from the bottom of the mound ditch. The resulting ground level of the mound-top seems to have sloped upwards away from the entrance, so that the eastern side of the keep, which was most exposed to mining attacks, was buried more deeply than the western side next the bailey. The presence of this fine gravel would have made mining from the side of the mound almost impossible, as any gallery driven through such loose soil would be almost certain to collapse unless it were very efficiently shored up.

Within the keep, the foundation storey was filled to a depth of about twelve feet, which represents, approximately, the average depth to which the exterior of the tower was buried. On the surface of the interior filling was laid the basement floor, formed of rammed lime. A few small portions of this remained adhering to the walls.

The basement floor contained two rooms, the eastern being thirty-four feet long by thirteen and the western twenty-nine feet long and of the same width as its neighbour, to which it was joined by a doorway, five and a half feet wide, passing through the cross wall. At the north-eastern corner of the west chamber, a lobby six feet wide led to the foot of the newel stair, a fine feature of the keep, thirteen feet wide. One of the steps was found, and showed the newel to have been a foot wide and the stair to have risen sixteen six-inch steps to the circuit. The lower part of the stair was filled up in comparatively recent times and a fireplace built in it.

The stair was lit by small windows (one of which remains) formed to pass out in the centre of the north central pilaster. The east chamber had two windows, to-day much broken, but having originally steeply sloping stepped internal sills and segmental rere-vaults. The west chamber probably also had two similar windows, but only the northern half of the northern one remains, its head lying on the floor within the chamber.

In the north-western angle of the keep, at about thirteen feet above the basement floor, may be seen the remains of a latrine chamber (sometimes, incorrectly, called "garderobe") which seems to have originally been about twelve feet wide and eight feet long. It was lit by a window in the western face of the angle buttress, and in the north-east angle was a shaft descending more than forty feet into the mound.

The top of the ruined walls show no signs of the whereabouts of the first floor. It would seem probable, however, that the present wall-tops represent the level of the bearing of the floor-joists of the next storey, which would then be a foot or so above the top of the walls as they appear to-day, making the distance between basement and first floors about twenty feet (a very usual storey height in late keeps).

The curious undercutting of the keep walling is due to the efforts of the destroyers in 1766, who thus endeavoured to overthrow the walls. They succeeded in overturning the west wall, which lay in three large fragments between the keep and the gatehouse. In their fall they had buried themselves deeply in the loose gravel of the mound-top, having to be dug out and removed with explosives. The disturbance of the ground at their fall and the subsequent turning over of the soil by the workmen who had hacked at them to take the material had made it impossible to attempt stratification in this area. Smaller portions of the west wall and cross-wall still lie within the keep on the gravel filling of its interior.

The Forebuilding

To the south of the keep, and of one build with it, is the forebuilding or entrance tower. This structure is of unusual size, being thirty-eight feet long and twenty-feet projection from the keep. Its walls are eight feet thick, the eastern being rather more. The exterior has a simple plinth, the burial of which under the gravel filling suggests that the latter was an afterthought and not part of the original scheme.

The interior of the forebuilding was not filled, its floor, of rammed lime, having thus been some eleven feet below that of the keep itself. The basement of the forebuilding was clearly a prison. It has no entrance, its occupants having probably been lowered through a trap in the floor above. In the south-west angle was a latrine (or "garderobe") which discharged directly into a cess-pit, seven feet by five, roofed with a barrel-vault and descending for an indeterminable depth into the mound. The oaken seat of the latrine (see Fig. IX) was discovered on the floor of the forebuilding during excavation and was found to fit exactly the slots provided for its reception in the sides of the latrine recess.

The manner in which the south wall of the forebuilding has broken away suggests that the prison was lit by a small window high up on this side.

The purpose of the curious holes cut in the walls of the prison remains a mystery. (See Fig.VIII).

High up in the south wall of the keep may be seen a beam-hole which demonstrates the level of the first floor of the forebuilding, which was thus twenty-four feet above its basement and perhaps seven feet below the corresponding floor of the keep.

In the angle between the east wall of the forebuilding and the south wall of the keep would have been the great stair, but excavation has not yet reached this point. A short stair would presumably have passed through the south wall of the keep joining the entrance floor of the forebuilding with the corresponding floor of the tower itself.

The entrance floor of the forebuilding would appear to have had in it a latrine chamber corresponding with that in the prison beneath, as a shaft passes down through the wall to discharge into the cess-pit already described.

There are a number of forebuildings in the country which are more elaborate than that of Bungay. Some of them include the great stair itself and are further elaborated to provide additional defences to this. The Bungay forebuilding, however, is merely a simple room, and, as such, is by far the largest structure in the country.

In its simplest form, the forebuilding is a small tower about twenty feet wide and with quite thin walls, forming as it were a protected quarter-landing to the great stair before the main door of the keep. If the little tower is not square, its projection is usually greater than its width. (See plan of Scarborough, Fig. XVI). At Bungay, however, we have a long tower covering a good deal of the south wall of the keep, providing more accommodation than was really necessary for a simple forebuilding. Its walls are thick, suggesting that it was a lofty structure.

It will be noticed that the axis of the keep is not the same as that of the original castle (see Figs. I and II), but is slewed round so that the keep is almost fore-square with the points of the compass. This has the effect of orientating the forebuilding, and I would therefore suggest that the floor over the entrance storey of this interesting tower was a chapel.

MINE GALLERY

The mine gallery beneath the south-western angle of the keep was described in the last part of the S.I.A. Proceedings (see page 26). It would appear reasonably certain that the gallery dates from the time of the surrender of the castle to Henry II in 1174.

Architectural Details

(See Figs. XI and XIII). Fig. XIa shows a section of a portion of moulded string built into the northern end of the west face of the keep basement. It is evidently re-used material from the destroyed stone hall and appears to be of the first half of the twelfth century.

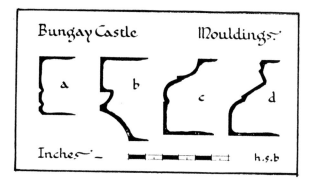

Fig. XI

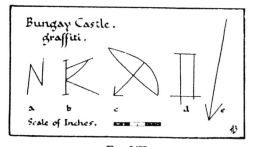

Fig. XII

Fig. XIII displays some of the architectural details found during the excavations. From left to right, first may be seen some of the stones from the keep plinth, the angle of slope being nine vertical to five horizontal.

Next is part of an impost moulding (section shown on Fig. XIb). This section is often found in connection with scalloped capitals, and it may be that the stone is an abacus of one of the capitals to the columns described below.

FIG. XIII — BUNGAY CASTLE
ARCHITECTURAL DETAILS FOUND DURING THE EXCAVATIONS.

FIG. XIV — BUNGAY CASTLE
STONES HAVING GRAFFITI UPON THEM.

Several stones were discovered which had formed part of a column or columns about two feet four inches in diameter. Portions of their bases were also discovered (Fig. XIII). Two different mouldings were found, their sections being shown on Fig. XIc and d). A very small portion was found of a scalloped capital which had also belonged to a column of about the same diameter (Fig. XIII).

The capital, bases and impost moulding all seem to belong to about the middle of the second half of the twelfth century.

It would seem that these columns can only belong to the keep, unless the estimated date of this structure (v. inf.) is very much out. The large diameter of the columns suggests that they formed part of an arcade taking the place of the cross-wall at the main floor level, as at Rochester keep (v. inf.). As there are two base sections, there may have been such an arcade on two floors (possibly the entrance floor as well as the main floor, or else an upper floor over the latter).

The portion of capital shown on Fig. XIII is resting on a stone which shows sections of vaulting shafts, the central of these being $5\frac{1}{8}$ inches and the two lateral $3\frac{3}{4}$ inches in diameter. This stone has come from a room vaulted in at least two bays of quadripartite vaulting, properly constructed with transverse rib and diagonal ribs. It is difficult to imagine which portion of the keep this might be; possibly one of the storeys of the forebuilding (? the chapel) may have been vaulted.

At the extreme right of the display of architectural details shown on Fig. XIII are three of the score or so of stones found which have formed part of an angle having a shaft eight inches in diameter running up it.

GRAFFITI

A number of graffiti or "mason marks" have been noted on the dressed stones found in the ruins. These are shown in Figs. XII and XIV.

The "N" or "lightning flash" (Fig. XIIa) appears on the vaulting-shaft stone and on an unmoulded stone. (Fig. XIV).

The mysterious sign XIIb (which may have been drawn upside-down) appears on a stone which is probably part of a salient angle of a doorway.

The bow with an arrow on the stave instead of the string (XIIc) appears on one of the stones of the keep plinth. (I understand that this sign is of common occurrence).

The "box" (XIId) is on an unmoulded stone.

The arrow or "spear" (XIIe) which may be upside down, appears on two unmoulded stones.*

At the top left-hand corner of Fig. XIV is shown a stone having two curved scratches which may be accidental.

PETROLOGY

The core of the walling of the keep consists of flint rubble.

The keep was faced internally and externally with a rubble casing of an estaurine sandstone probably from the moors behind Scarborough. This stone is similar to the Aislaby stone used for some of the Yorkshire abbeys built during the second half of the twelfth century.

The shafted quoin-stones are of an oolitic limestone of the Barnack-Ketton type.

The remainder of the dressed stones are of Caen stone.

I am indebted to the Director of the Geological Survey for assistance in connection with the elucidation of the sources of the stones and also to Professor Pruvost of Lille University, to whom I sent some samples in case they might have been quarried on the Continent.

DATE OF THE KEEP

The earliest keeps in this country, the "hall-keeps," were large, two-storeyed structures having a great hall and a great chamber placed side by side and raised above a storage basement. East Anglian examples are Norwich and Castle Rising. About 1125 the hall-keeps began to give place to the "tower-keeps" which were smaller, loftier towers having the chamber situated over the hall instead of alongside it. Sometimes there was also a separate entrance floor, as at Hedingham in Essex.

The hall-keeps had walls about eight to ten feet thick and their chief external ornamentation was thin pilaster strips passing up their walls. With the raising of the towers their walls became thicker and strong basements were instituted as protection against mining. By the middle of the twelfth century the narrow pilaster strip was

*One of which was inadvertently built into the restored south-west angle of the keep in 1935.

The Keep of Bungay Castle in Suffolk.

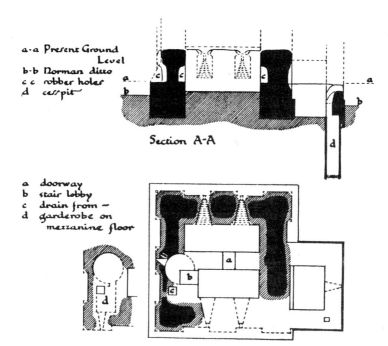

a·a Present Ground
 Level
b·b Norman ditto
c c robber holes
d   cesspit

Section A-A

a   doorway
b   stair lobby
c   drain from —
d   garderobe on
    mezzanine floor

Basement Plan

N

a·a Mine Gallery
b   Prison
c   Garderobe
d   Cesspit

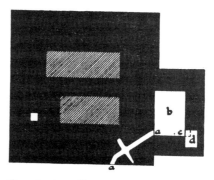

Foundation Plan

Scale of Feet

10   0   50   100

FIG. XV

giving place to the broader form which had originally been designed to provide space for the angle-staircases in the thin walls of the hall-keeps. (Compare Norwich with later Rising).

The square plan and thick walls of Bungay keep show it to belong to the second type of keep and the discovery of the broad pilasters suggest that it is fairly late in date. Another fact which points to a late date is the elaborate forebuilding already noted. At the outset, therefore, we may suggest a mid-twelfth century origin for Bungay keep.

The earliest known keep which has broad pilasters in place of the narrow strip type is the fine tower of Scarborough, begun by Henry II in 1157. This keep has also the peculiarity of a staircase away from the angle, as at Bungay. No other keep has this feature, so that there is a very close link in this respect between the two keeps. It would seem reasonable to suppose that a private keep would have been behind, rather than ahead, of the fashion set by the royal engineers, so perhaps we may assume Bungay keep to have been built later than 1157.

In the summer of that year, Hugh Bigod was deprived of his castles, not getting them back until 1163, when Henry had become involved in a dispute with Thomas Becket and was trying to win the lay lords to his cause. Bungay keep could not have been built in the period 1157–63, as no accounts concerning it appear in the Great Roll of the Pipe.

It may therefore be a reasonable supposition that Hugh Bigod commenced the keep soon after getting Bungay Castle back in 1163. He could not have built it much later, as it would have taken many years to build, and he was finally deprived of the castle in 1174. Moreover, in 1165, we find Henry starting his favourite castle of Orford, apparently for the purpose of keeping Bigod and his Flemish mercenaries in check. The design of Orford keep shows a considerable advance on that of Bungay, so it would seem probable that the initiation of the latter antedates that of Orford.

The probable date of foundation of Bungay keep is thus suggested as about 1163–5.

It is not impossible that the keep may have been built before 1157, but it must have taken many, perhaps eight or ten, years to build, and the mouldings, as well as the segmental heads to the basement windows, do not suggest such an early date as 1150. Very few tower-keeps in this country are datable from documentary evidence, and very little work has been done in connection with the examination of Norman castles which provides much assistance in dating their features from architectural evidence.

It has been suggested that the Anarchy of Stephen's reign, with its forced labour of peasantry, may have produced some of the keeps in this country. The wail of the Anglo-Saxon Chronicle — "They cruelly oppressed the wretched men of the land with castle-works" — may refer to the building of keeps, but may equally be referring to earth and timber castles. In any case, the same might possibly have been said of Hugh Bigod's reign in East Anglia until Henry II finished his career in 1174.

It may be that future research will ante-date the period *c.*1164 suggested as the date of commencement for Bungay Keep, but I feel that the extraordinary resemblance between this keep and that of Scarborough is too remarkable not to serve as some indication.

A point which may be followed up by future students is the interesting one of the origin of the rubble with which the keep was faced. William d'Aumale, Earl of York and lord of the (then keep-less) castle of Scarborough, appears to have been a friend of Hugh Bigod during the Anarchy, and thus may have provided the latter Earl with stone for a castle, which Bigod would not have found so easy to procure after Henry had turned d'Aumale out of Scarborough in 1155, and thereafter constructed the royal keep in that castle. On the other hand, it is equally probable that the rubble is re-used material from the stone hall which certainly preceded the keep and which may have been built during the Anarchy.

COMPARISON OF THE KEEPS OF BUNGAY AND SCARBOROUGH AND ATTEMPTED RESTORATION OF THE FORMER BY ANALOGY WITH THE LATTER.

See Figs. XVI and XVII. Scarborough Keep, commenced about 1157 by Henry II after he had subdued William d'Aumale, Earl of York, and taken his castle from him in 1155, is a rather smaller tower than that of Bungay, the solid "anti-mine" base of the latter being seventy feet square to the sixty-three of the Yorkshire tower. In both cases the thickness of wall in the foundation is eighteen feet.

The habitable basement storey, at which level the two plans on Fig. XVI are taken, have walls thirteen feet thick in both keeps, the plinths in both cases projecting five feet and sloping at an angle slightly less than sixty degrees with the horizontal. (Actually nine vertical to five horizontal).

While the two plans compared on Fig. XVI show clearly their family resemblance, their minor differences seem to be due mainly to their unequal sizes. Thus, while the pilaster strips ornamenting Scarborough vary from nine to twelve feet wide and project only a foot, those of the larger tower are eleven to thirteen feet wide and of two feet projection. The greater internal span of Bungay keep necessitated the provision of a cross-wall to assist in carrying the floors; at Scarborough the span was unbroken in the basement and on the upper floor, where the thinning of the walls had increased the span, a great arch spanned the interior in place of a cross-wall.

In both keeps the circular stair is away from the angle, a remarkable eccentricity already noted. At Scarborough the stair is in the thickness of a side wall and is twelve feet in diameter, at Bungay the cross-wall assists in housing the stair, which seems to have been thirteen feet in diameter.

In both keeps the "anti-mine" basement is filled with soil and the lower stage of the forebuilding left empty but inaccessible, to serve as a pit-prison. Both prisons have a latrine with a vaulted cesspit, and both were lit by a loop high up in the wall away from the main tower.

The Scarborough forebuilding is of the small, rather primitive, type with thin walls and having its projection as the larger horizontal dimension. It had, however, three floors, the upper of which, over the entrance, may have been a chapel. The Bungay forebuilding, described in a previous section of this report, is very large and has unusually thick walls, and has been prolonged as noted along the wall of the main tower, possibly so as to provide room for a commodious chapel on its upper floor.

It will be noted that the great stair to the forebuilding, seen on the plan of Scarborough keep, has not yet been found at Bungay.

Another feature which suggests that Bungay keep post-dates that of Scarborough is not shown on the comparative plans. The latrine shoots in the main tower at Bungay were constructed to discharge into the mound without passing into the open air, whereas at Scarborough the more primitive method was employed of letting them discharge through the external wall-face between the pilasters and down the sloping plinth.

The angles of the latter keep are ornamented with shafts running

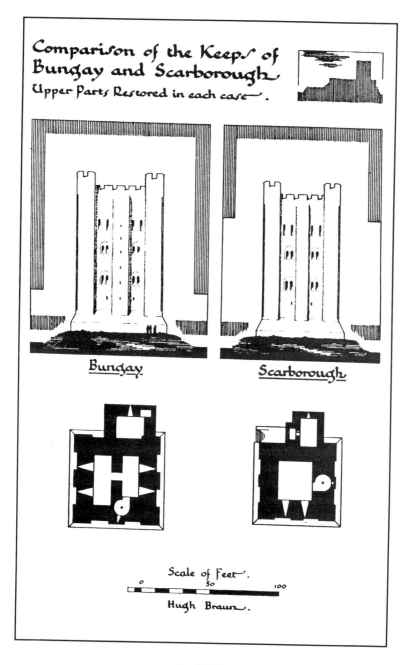

FIG. XVI

up them. The discovery of shafted quoin-stones at Bungay suggests a similar feature.

Let us now consider the section of Scarborough keep and see how that of Bungay may have resembled it. From this comparison we may be able to obtain some impression of the original appearance of the great East Anglian tower.

The earth-filled "anti-mine" basement at Bungay is about twelve feet deep. The depth of the corresponding basement at Scarborough has not been ascertained, but it is at least ten feet deep.

The basement proper at Scarborough is just under twenty feet in height, and the height of the corresponding storey at Bungay appears to have been about the same.

The windows lighting each of the floors at Bungay keep were probably in the east and west walls, two windows lighting each half of the tower.

The entrance floor at Scarborough is about twenty feet in height, has four windows and a fireplace. In it is the main door of the keep, at the head of a short stair leading from the rather lower floor of the forebuilding. The same could probably have been said concerning the entrance floor of Bungay keep. At Scarborough, however, the place of the cross-wall has been taken by a huge arch spanning right across the keep and helping to support the floor over. The cross-wall was presumably omitted because the floor was required as one room.

The second floor of the tower-keep was usually the Great Hall. At Scarborough this storey was again twenty feet high, but was divided into two rooms by a cross-wall, which makes its purpose rather difficult to conjecture. One of the rooms has a fireplace in it, and it may be that this storey contained private rooms of the castellan, the great hall of the tower being in the entrance storey. This seems probable when we observe that the uppermost storey, which is usually that containing the Great Chamber of the castellan, has no fireplace — an essential feature of such an apartment.

It would thus seem possible that the great hall of the keep was on the entrance floor and that both the two uppermost floors were given over to the private apartments of the castellan. The top storey at Scarborough was also about twenty feet high to the springing of the roof, this having been probably in two spans with a pitch of about fifty degrees.

The probable arrangement of the cross-wall at Bungay presents difficulties. The actual span along the length of this wall is twenty-nine feet, the same as that at Scarborough, where it is spanned by the great arch. At Hedingham in Essex there is also a great arch spanning the interior of the keep, and this too has a span of the same width. It is therefore tempting to suppose that Bungay also had a single great arch, a much better arrangement than the more primitive arcade at Rochester, a very early tower-keep begun in 1128. On the other hand, the discovery of the portions of large columns lends support to the arcade idea, especially as the cross-wall in the basement is such a very sturdy construction. (There may, however, have been half-round responds with scalloped capitals at the springing of the arch, as at Hedingham). It is to be hoped that future excavation will produce evidence of the form taken by the cross-wall.

By analogy with Scarborough, it may be supposed that the keep of Bungay also had four storeys. Above the existing basement may

Fig. XVII — Bungay Castle
The Keep restored. South-west aspect

have been an entrance floor twenty feet high, a second floor of the same height and an upper floor twenty feet high to the springing of the roof. This makes a height of eighty feet from the basement floor to the springing of the roof, this having probably been in two spans of perhaps fifty degrees pitch, making the ridges about sixteen feet above the springing. The wall-walk would probably have been at about the level of the ridges, and thus about ninety-six feet above the basement floor. The crenellated parapet would have been at least six feet in height, making the whole height of the tower about 102 feet above the basement floor. The angles would certainly have been taken up as turrets, probably ten feet higher than the tower itself. Thus the total height may have been about 112 feet above the basement floor — or 124 feet above the foundations of this mighty tower. Even if the keep had only possessed three floors, the minimum accommodation for a tower-keep, only twenty feet need be taken from these heights. The Great Tower of Bungay may thus take its place among the loftiest keeps in the country.

Cost of the Keep

The cost of some of the twelfth-century keeps may be ascertained from the building accounts still to be seen in the Great Roll of the Pipe. From these figures and a study of the plans of the towers themselves I have been able to arrive at an approximate "cubic rate" for mid-twelfth century Norman keeps in England. At a rough estimate, I should imagine that Bungay keep would have cost about £1,400 Norman, say £35,000 of our money to-day. Even if the keep had only been three storeys high, thus reducing the cost to, say, £30,000, we can quite appreciate the willingness of Hugh Bigod to pay a thousand marks — about £15,000 to-day — to save his great tower from destruction.

The Inner Gatehouse

After the surrender of the Castle in 1174 and its consequent seizure by the Crown, there is at present a gap in our knowledge of the history of the place. The reversion to the Bigods took place soon after the accession of Richard I in 1189, but it seems that the new lord of the Bigod estates, Roger, the son of Hugh the Restless, gave his attention primarily to rebuilding the much more commodious castle at Framlingham, building there the lofty towered curtains which remain in such good preservation to-day.

The period at which the curtain wall surrounding the mound-top at Bungay was erected is not at present clear, but it would appear that at some time during the thirteenth century the upper part of the obsolete keep was taken down and its materials employed in building the new curtains.

The entrance through these high walls, which are about six and a half feet in thickness and have the wall-walk about twenty-six feet above the level of the mound, at the remaining western side of the enclosure, was by a twin-towered gatehouse of simple plan. Two half-round towers, twenty-two feet in diameter, rise above square bases on either side of the entrance passage, which is ten feet wide between the flanks of the towers. The tower-bases are of solid masonry, and their walls above vary from seven to ten feet in thickness, according to the amount to which the wall-face was exposed to assault.

Internally, the towers are only six feet across and open at the gorge, but the upper stage of each once had a small room, formed by carrying a light wall across the gorge on an arch. (A portion of this wall was found lying at the foot of the north tower). These rooms, which were about twelve feet high, were entered from the wall-walks through simple unmoulded pointed arches and vaulted lobbies, and the two rooms were joined by short stairs passing through the internal walls to the roof over the central portion of the gatehouse. Why this roof was at a higher level does not seem apparent, as there are no indications of a chamber over the entrance, nor does it seem possible for such to have been accessible. Possibly the way to the tower-tops was from the roof of the central portion of the gatehouse. The roof of the central portion appears to have been about thirty-two feet above the entrance passage and the roofs of the towers were perhaps some six feet higher.

The walls of the towers are unpierced externally.

BRIDGE-PIT

One of the most interesting features exposed during the excavations is the pit which housed the mechanism of the "turning-bridge,"

FIG. XVIII — BUNGAY CASTLE. The Bridge-pit, showing the Chases for the Counterpoise, one of the Socket-holes for the Axle, and the Scoop at the Back of the Pit to allow for the Turning of the Bridge.

and which, when this was up, barred access to the innermost enclosure of the castle. (Fig. XVIII). Very few of these pits have been excavated, and probably none shows the arrangements so perfectly as the example at Bungay.

The deep ditch in front of the gatehouse was spanned by a permanent wooden bridge, which terminated on a stone pier joining the outer faces of the twin towers. The square bases of these towers project some twelve feet in front of the main wall of the gatehouse, and between this and their internal flanks is the deep pit which separated the last pier of the permanent bridge from the threshold of the gate. The sides of the pit are carried up by the cheeks of the steep talus from which each tower rises, and which assists the change from square base to semi-circular tower proper. The lower part of each tower and the face of its talus is of good ashlar, the stone being oolitic limestone. Above this, the masonry is of flint rubble faced with sandstone rubble spoil from the keep. Much of the stonework of the gatehouse, apart from the bases referred to above, is re-used stones from the Norman building.

The bridge-pit is about ten feet square, and presumably passed down to the scarp of the ditch beneath. (Excavation has been stopped, however, at a level of about ten feet below the entrance passage). The back of the pit is roughly level with the front of the gatehouse proper, the portion of this below the entrance passage being of solid masonry, in which may be seen the chases for the counterpoise of the bridge (Fig. XVIII). At the sides of the pit are rough holes about a foot square, which once held the axle of the bridge. The present condition of the holes is somewhat puzzling. As they now appear a beam could not have turned in them. Either the actual socket stones have been removed, which seems most probable, or else the axle was a fixed beam, round which the bridge turned, which would have been an unusual arrangement. At the level of the centres of the holes, a small set-off passes along the sides of the pit. (In the drawing of the attempted reconstruction of the bridge (Fig. XIX) I have suggested that this set-off was carried across the bridge-pier and formed the bearing of the outer end of the bridge). The south side of the pit is not vertical, but slopes as a sort of battering plinth to the tower. This batter is stopped before the axle-hole is reached, and was obviously intended to serve as a check to the counterpoise when the bridge rose, so that its upper surface would not bump against the front of the gate-arch.

The floor of the entrance passage was decked over with balks of timber, six inches thick, which also covered the chases for the counterpoise. That this decking was permanent is shown by the fact that the timbers were built-in, the upper walling actually standing upon them. This may account for the bad condition of the walling of the entrance passage, which has nearly all collapsed, making the original plan difficult to elucidate. Indeed, the whole of the passage between the flanks of the towers has been swept clean, possibly when the gatehouse was turned into a cottage at the end of the eighteenth century. There is thus practically no trace of the entrance arch, except for a few sorry scraps of re-used stones marking its site. The walls of the entrance passage appear to have been patched from time to time, possibly due to the failure of the timber decking referred to above.

The thickness of the entrance arch cannot be ascertained, but some idea as to the site of the great door may be obtained by inspecting the remains of the hole for the locking-bar which passes right through the wall of the south tower. The sides of this hole have been very much robbed, but its original site may be guessed at. Above is another small hole which must have had something to do with the door, being possibly the sill of a fixed wooden tympanum filling up the arch above the hinged valves of the door below. This upper hole is roughly level with the string-course which caps the ashlar bases of the towers and which probably marks the springing-line of the entrance arch.

The timber floor does not appear to have reached the back of the pit, but stopped, apparently, at the back of the entrance arch, that is to say, at the site of the great door. The place of the decking was probably taken, at this point, by a stone kerb forming the front of the landing between the chases, and serving to protect the edge of the decking and prevent it from slipping forward. The edge is now too broken away for it to be certain as to what happened at this point.

The Turning-Bridge

Nothing appears to be known about these interesting examples of mediæval engineering, and it may perhaps be of interest to attempt to reconstruct the Bungay bridge from the traces remaining of its site (Fig. XIX).

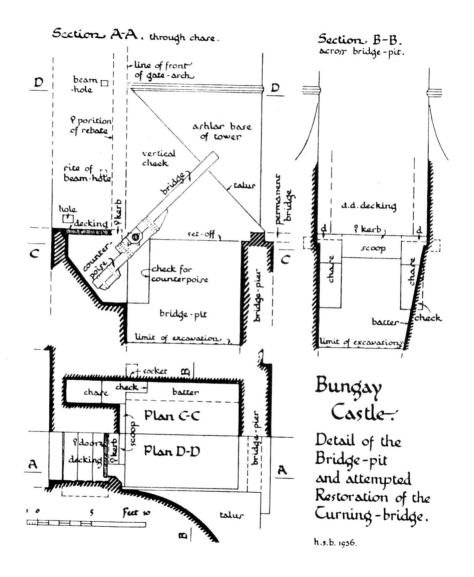

Section A-A. through chase.

Section B-B. across bridge-pit.

D · beam-hole · line of front of gate-arch · D

? position of rebate · ashlar base of tower · vertical check

site of beam-hole · bridge · talus · permanent bridge

hole · decking · ? kerb · counterpoise · set-off

C · check for counterpoise · C

bridge-pit · bridge-pier

limit of excavation ?

d.d. decking · d · ? kerb · d

chase · scoop · chase

batter · check

limit of excavation?

socket · check · batter

chase · Plan C-C

? door · decking · ? kerb · scoop · Plan D-D · bridge-pier

A · A

talus

0 · 5 · feet · 10

Bungay Castle.

Detail of the Bridge-pit and attempted Restoration of the Turning-bridge.

h.s.b. 1936.

Fig. XIX

The manner in which it was pivoted is not quite certain (v. sup.) but the site of its bearings is approximately ascertainable.

If the ledge at the sides of the pit represents the level of the outer bearing, it would appear that the main beams of the bridge were designed partly to rest upon the axle and partly notched or tenoned into it. It is clear that these beams could not have projected inwards to form the counterpoise, as the decking above the chases is not high enough to allow of this. It would seem, therefore, that the counterpoise beams were separate and joined to the bridge-beams in the manner suggested on the drawing (Fig. XIX). The actual weights may have been of pig-iron attached to the ends of the arms.

The bridge was apparently designed so as the counterpoise just mastered the bridge itself, that is to say, the normal position of the bridge was "up." This is suggested by the check for the counterpoise noted above, and would, indeed, seem a reasonable supposition in any case, and suitable to the requirements of the defenders. The counterpoise arms being inaccessible by reason of the decking, the bridge must have therefore been secured at its outer end. This could easily have been effected by employing small weights, such as a couple of pieces of stone or boxes of earth. In time of need, the last retreating defenders could kick away the weights and make their way along the bridge into the gatehouse, the bridge, relieved of their weight, rising behind them, and taking up its position in front of the gate-arch. The bridge could easily be lowered from within by pushing it until a person could stand upon it and walk out to the end, the bridge falling beneath his weight until it was down and could be secured as suggested above.

A mysterious feature is the hole shown on the drawing just above the inner edge of the gatehouse decking. This hole is fifteen inches deep and appears to have held a beam which could be removed at will, the hole on the opposite side of the passage being slotted backwards for the purpose. What such a beam could have been for is a mystery, as it would pass across the entrance and interfere with traffic, but the whole back of the gatehouse has been so much altered and damaged that nothing can be very certain about any of its details.

DATE OF THE GATEHOUSE

The problem of the date of the gatehouse, and the curtain-walls, which are of one build with it, presents some difficulty.

It is known that Roger Bigod obtained a licence to crenellate his *"mansum"* of "Bungeye" in Suffolk in 1294, and in the absence of any other evidence, it would seem reasonable to suppose that the high walls and gatehouse are of that date. On the other hand, however, a distinguished antiquary with much knowledge of military architecture, visited Bungay Castle during the summer of 1935 and expressed his surprise that the gatehouse could have been erected so late as 1294, as, had he not heard of the licence, he would have dated it as nearer 1200. Upon reflection, I could not help appreciating his views as regards the date, and feel, therefore, that it would perhaps be as well to consider the design of the gatehouse in detail before accepting the date 1294.

The twin-towered gatehouse appears in this country during the last quarter of the twelfth century and by the end of the century the towers are nearly always semi-circular, the vulnerable corners of the early square type having been done away with.

For the first quarter of the thirteenth century, the towers remain backless, until the military architects realised the possibilities of having floors from which archers could shoot at the enemy through arrow-slits in the walls of the towers. In general design, therefore, the gatehouse might be of the first quarter of the thirteenth century. In defence of the 1294 theory, however, I would suggest that the reason for the primitive plan of the towers is that they are so small internally that rooms in their lower storeys would only be six feet in diameter and were thus not worth having. (The walls are thinned down considerably to provide space for the upper rooms). The castle was so small that there would have been no room for larger towers. The little half-hexagon wall-tower south of the keep certainly looks most primitive, resembling the towers of Framlingham, erected about 1190. Nothing but the plan of this is known, however, so it cannot be adequately discussed.

My attention was also drawn to the very primitive looking string-course which caps the ashlar bases of the gate-towers (the only architectural detail the gatehouse possess). At first glance this resembles the late twelfth-century moulding which may be seen in the aisles of the Abbey Church at Fountains in Yorkshire. Upon comparison, however, I found that the two mouldings, were quite different, that at Fountains having a broad vertical face and much less steep chambers than the string at Bungay, which shows comparatively little vertical face. Up to the present I have been able to find no moulding comparable with the Bungay string-course, but I am satisfied that it need not necessarily be of late-twelfth century date.

The chief feature of the Bungay gatehouse is, of course, the "turning-bridge". The earliest form of moveable bridge was the "draw-bridge" (*pons tractilis*), where, I suppose, the bridge was simply drawn back horizontally, possibly plank by plank, into the castle. The next form was the "turning-bridge" (*pons tornatilis* or sometimes *versatilis*), which is the type under consideration.

The earliest mention of a "turning-bridge" I have been able to discover is that noted, to be built at Winchester Castle, in the Close Roll for 1235. Baxter and Johnston's "Mediæval Latin Words" gives the earliest reference as 1220. The type certainly goes on into the fourteenth century, being replaced towards the middle of that century by the *"pons levabilis"*, the ordinary "lifting-bridge" familiar to most of us, and in use in various forms down to the last century. The period at which the "turning-bridge" seems to have been most popular was the middle of the thirteenth-century. The excellent example recently discovered in the barbican of the Tower of London, interesting by reason of its three counterpoise chases, seems to have been constructed soon after 1274, as the barbican ditch was being finished at that date. This pit, although more finely finished, and in better masonry, than the Bungay example, is without the latter's refinement of the check to the bridge counterpoise, which suggests that the Bungay pit is an improved version of that at London, and therefore of later date. (It may be of interest to note that Hugh Bigod, father of that Roger Bigod who in 1294 obtained the Bungay licence, had been for a while Governor of the Tower of London, having been appointed in 1258).

In the absence of any irrefutable evidence to the contrary, it seems that we must accept the date of the "licence to crenellate" — 1294 — as being the date of the curtain-walls and inner gatehouse of Bungay Castle.

THE INNER BAILEY AND ITS GATEHOUSE

Experimental soundings made during the recent excavations determined the site and probable form of the gatehouse to the Inner Bailey. It seems to have been a twin-towered structure similar to the

Inner Gatehouse, possibly being contemporary with it. It is greatly
to be hoped that an attempt will be made at some future date to
investigate the whole of this bailey. Much of its curtain wall
remains, in a shocking condition, however, being overgrown with
vegetation to such an extent as to be almost invisible. It is to be
hoped that these old walls may be cleaned and preserved and it
might even be found possible to conduct inexpensive excavations
within the bailey to recover the plan of the Great Hall and other
domestic buildings of Bungay Castle.